The Atlantic Ocean

by Anne Ylvisaker

Consultant:
Sarah E. Schoedinger
Education Coordinator
Consortium for Oceanographic Research and Education
Washington, D.C.

Bridgestone Books

an imprint of Capstone Press
Mankato, Minnesota

Bridgestone Books are published by Capstone Press
151 Good Counsel Drive, P.O. Box 669, Mankato, Minnesota 56002
http://www.capstone-press.com

Library of Congress Cataloging-in-Publication Data
Ylvisaker, Anne.
    The Atlantic Ocean / by Anne Ylvisaker.
    p. cm.—(Oceans)
    Includes bibliographical references and index.
    Summary: Introduces the long, curving ocean that covers approximately one fifth
of the earth's surface, and provides instructions for an activity to demonstrate evaporation
of saltwater.
    ISBN 0-7368-1424-8 (hardcover)
    1. Oceanography—Atlantic Ocean—Juvenile literature. [1. Atlantic Ocean.
2. Oceanography.] I. Title.
GC481 .Y58 2003
551.46'1—dc21   2001007908

Editorial Credits
Megan Schoeneberger, editor; Karen Risch, product planning editor; Linda Clavel,
    designer; Image Select International, photo researcher

Photo Credits
Corbis/Stephen Frink, 18; Digital Vision, 14; Digital Wisdom/Mountain High, 6, 8 (map);
Erin Scott/SARIN Creative, 10; ImageState, 16, 20; Masterfile, 12; PhotoDisc, Inc., cover, 4;
Rod Catanach, Woods Hole Oceanographic Institution, 8 (photo); RubberBall Productions,
22, 23

Table of Contents

The Atlantic Ocean

The Atlantic Ocean is the second largest ocean. It takes up almost one-fifth of Earth's surface. The Atlantic covers more than 31 million square miles (80 million square kilometers). It is nearly six and one-half times the size of the United States.

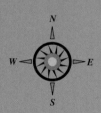

Atlantic Ocean

Other water areas

ARCTIC
OCEAN

NORTH
AMERICA

EUROPE

ATLANTIC OCEAN

SARGASSO SEA

AFRICA

PACIFIC OCEAN

INDIAN
OCEAN

SOUTH
AMERICA

N

W *E*

S

6

ANTARCTIC OCEAN

Location of the Atlantic Ocean

The Atlantic Ocean is shaped a little like the letter *S*. The continents of North America and South America border the Atlantic on the west. Europe and Africa form the eastern border. The Atlantic reaches from the Arctic Ocean to the Antarctic Ocean.

continent
one of the seven main landmasses of Earth

Scientists use submersibles (suhb-MUHR-si-buhls) to study deep water. This underwater machine is called *ALVIN*. Scientists use *ALVIN* to study the deepest parts of the Atlantic.

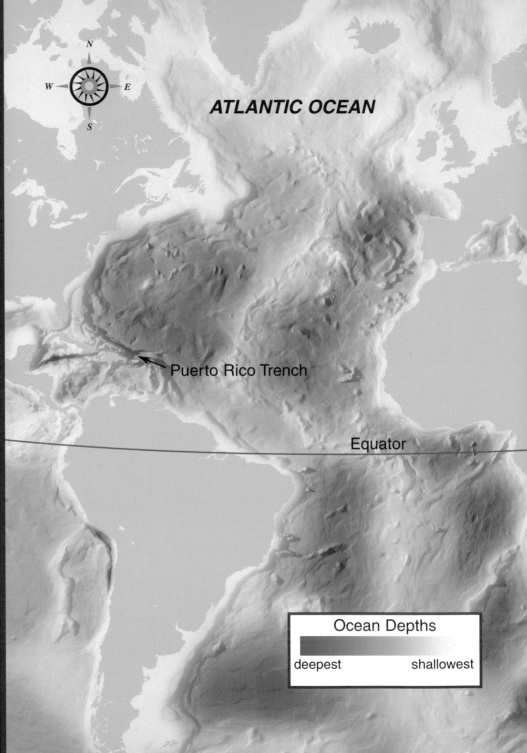

ATLANTIC OCEAN

N
W · E
S

Puerto Rico Trench

Equator

Ocean Depths

deepest   shallowest

Depth of the Atlantic Ocean

The average depth of the Atlantic Ocean is about 12,000 feet (3,700 meters). This depth is about 2 miles (3 kilometers). The deepest place in the Atlantic is the Puerto Rico Trench. There, the Atlantic is more than 5 miles (8 kilometers) deep.

depth
a measure of how
deep something is

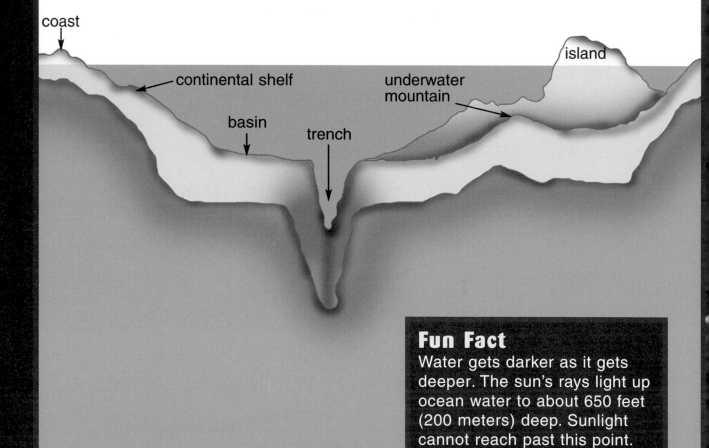

coast

island

continental shelf

underwater
mountain

basin

trench

Fun Fact
Water gets darker as it gets
deeper. The sun's rays light up
ocean water to about 650 feet
(200 meters) deep. Sunlight
cannot reach past this point.

The Bottom of the Atlantic Ocean

The continental shelf slopes from the ocean's coast to the basin. The basin of the Atlantic Ocean has mountains, trenches, and flat areas. The Mid-Atlantic Ridge is an underwater mountain range. It is about 7,000 miles (11,300 kilometers) long. Its tallest peaks make islands.

basin
the low, flat part
of an ocean's floor

Fun Fact
The northern Atlantic Ocean has many large pieces of floating ice called icebergs. In 1912, the ship *Titanic* sank in the northern Atlantic after hitting an iceberg.

12

The Water in the Atlantic Ocean

Water in the Atlantic Ocean is saltier than the Pacific or the Indian Ocean. The water's temperature changes by location. It can be 86 degrees Fahrenheit (30 degrees Celsius) near the equator. It can be 28 degrees Fahrenheit (2 degrees Celsius below zero) in the north.

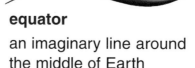

equator
an imaginary line around
the middle of Earth

The Climate around the Atlantic Ocean

The climate around the Atlantic Ocean changes by location. The area near the equator is hot year-round. The weather is colder in the north and south. The northern and southern parts of the Atlantic Ocean have long, cold winters.

climate
the usual weather that occurs in a place

Animals in the Atlantic Ocean

Many animals live in the Atlantic Ocean. Whales migrate between warm and cool areas of the Atlantic. Fish such as tuna swim in the Atlantic. Crabs, sea stars, and lobsters crawl on the ocean floor. Corals are small animals that make coral reefs in warm water.

migrate
to move from one place to another

Fun Fact
The Sargasso Sea is a large area in the western Atlantic Ocean. The water there is very still. The area is filled with a brown seaweed called sargassum weed.

Plants in the Atlantic Ocean

Ocean plants grow in shallow water. Seaweed grows in the ocean. Seaweed can be red, green, or brown. Tiny plants called phytoplankton float near the surface of the Atlantic Ocean. They are food for many ocean animals.

shallow
not deep

Keeping the Atlantic Ocean Healthy

The Atlantic Ocean is becoming polluted. Trash and fertilizers pollute lakes and rivers. The dirty water enters the ocean from rivers. Pollution kills plants and animals. People are working to keep the Atlantic Ocean clean.

fertilizer
something added to soil to grow bigger plants; some fertilizers can hurt ocean plants and animals.

21

Hands On: Gathering Salt from the Ocean

Some of the salt that people put on their food comes from the ocean. Salt water from the ocean is put in shallow pools in the sun. Water dries and leaves the salt behind. You can try this activity to see how it works.

What You Need

1 teaspoon (5 mL) salt
⅓ cup (75 mL) warm water
Small bowl
Spoon

What You Do

1. Stir the salt and water in the bowl.
2. Dip your finger into the water. Take a little taste. The salty water tastes like ocean water.
3. Put the dish in a sunny place.
4. Check on the water each day.

How long did it take for the water to dry? How much salt is left behind?

Words to Know

average (AV-uh-rij)—the most common amount of something; an average amount is found by adding figures together and dividing by the number of figures.

continental shelf (KON-tuh-nuhn-tuhl SHELF)—the shallow area of an ocean's floor near a coast

coral reef (KOR-uhl REEF)—an area of coral skeletons near the surface of an ocean

lobster (LOB-stur)—a sea creature with a hard shell and large claws

phytoplankton (FITE-oh-plangk-tuhn)—tiny plants that drift in oceans; phytoplankton are too small to be seen without a microscope; a microscope is a tool that makes things appear larger than they really are.

pollution (puh-LOO-shuhn)—materials that hurt Earth's water, air, and land

surface (SUR-fiss)—the top or outside layer of something

trench (TRENCH)—a long, narrow valley in an ocean

Read More

Heller, Ruth. *A Sea within a Sea: Secrets of the Sargasso.* New York: Grosset & Dunlap, 2000.

Petersen, David, and Christine Peterson. *The Atlantic Ocean.* A True Book. New York: Children's Press, 2001.

Taylor, L. R. (Leighton R.) *The Atlantic Ocean.* Life in the Sea. Woodbridge, Conn.: Blackbirch Press, 1999.

Internet Sites

Oceanlink
http://www.oceanlink.island.net
What's It Like Where You Live?—Temperate Oceans
http://mbgnet.mobot.org/salt/oceans

Index